DUBAI
THE CITY AT A GLANCE

CW00642929

Meydan Racecourse
This 60,000-seat arena sits in a 7.5
complex where one hotel has a tra(
A museum and corporate suites are
See p084

The Dubai Mall
In what is the world's largest mall (for now),
you can watch a film, dine, ice-skate, scuba-
dive and, of course, shop until you drop.
Doha Street, T 362 7500

The Address Downtown
Boasting a clutch of great restaurants, this
towering hotel has the best pool area in town.
See p020

Old Town
If you don't have much that is historic, why
not build something that looks as if it might
be? This mixed-use development is a meld
of pan-Arabian architectural influences.

Burj Khalifa
The world's highest tower is one of the most
beautiful pieces of architecture in the city.
See p065

Al Quoz
Throughout this industrial district, warehouses
are increasingly being turned into art galleries,
cultural collectives and studio spaces.

Dubai Marina
An Emerald City-esque cluster, the Marina has
a resort-like feel that attracts wealthy residents.
See p010

Burj Al Arab
WKK Architects' famously OTT hotel is one
of Dubai's most unmistakable landmarks.
See p013

INTRODUCTION

THE CHANGING FACE OF THE URBAN SCENE

Beneath its Middle Eastern veneer, Dubai is really Asian. Arabic is the national language and Islam is the official religion, but while you'll hear a *'salaam alaikum'* or two, Arabic is notable only for its absence. As are the Arabs. Emiratis account for about nine per cent of the population, South Asians for more than half.

A Gulf state with limited oil of its own, Dubai is an economic powerhouse. Poised between Iran, the still unstable Iraq, and the hard-line Islamic republic of Saudi Arabia, the city is open and fairly tolerant. It also has global clout, although its population is only two million. Admittedly, the plan to increase that total to five million and tourist arrivals to 15 million by 2010 failed, but talk is of getting there soon. Impossible? Maybe. But even after Dubai's near-collapse during the 2008 crisis, that's a word rarely heard in the city modesty never visited. Now the speed of development is picking up once again, it has resumed its vaulting ambitions.

Perhaps it's the squeaky-clean urban environment. Perhaps it's the good life. Whatever the draw, people keep coming. *Stepford Wives*-perfect, Dubai feels like a giant resort, at least the parts that aren't a construction site. Love it or loathe it, the city is a modern phenomenon that tempers its bad habits (it's unsustainable and fractured along class and racial lines) with a belief that everything can and should be changed. Dubai is all about upward mobility, and in a region currently in turmoil that alone makes it a marvel.

ESSENTIAL INFO
FACTS, FIGURES AND USEFUL ADDRESSES

TOURIST OFFICE
Visitor Information Bureau
Deira City Centre
T 282 1111
www.definitelydubai.com

TRANSPORT
Airport transfer to Downtown
The metro runs from Terminals 1 and 3
to Deira and along Sheikh Zayed Road
www.rta.ae
Car hire
Avis
T 224 5219
Public transport
www.rta.ae
Taxis
Dubai Taxi
T 208 0808
There are also cab ranks outside shopping
malls and the larger hotels

EMERGENCY SERVICES
Ambulance/Police
T 999
Fire
T 997
24-hour pharmacy
Binsina Pharmacy
Al Rigga Road
T 224 7650

EMBASSIES/CONSULATES
British Embassy
Al Seef Road
T 309 4444
www.gov.uk/government/world/
united-arab-emirates
US Consulate-General
Al Seef Road
T 309 4000
dubai.usconsulate.gov

POSTAL SERVICES
Post office
Abu Hail Road
T 262 2222
Shipping
UPS
T 339 1939
www.ups.com

BOOKS
The Architecture of the United Arab
Emirates by Salma Samar Damluji
(Garnet Publishing)
Dubai Architecture & Design
edited by Sabina Marreiros (Daab)

WEBSITES
Art
www.thethirdline.com
Newspaper
www.thenational.ae

EVENTS
Art Dubai
www.artdubai.ae
Design Days
www.designdaysdubai.ae
Downtown Design
www.downtowndesign.com

COST OF LIVING
Taxi from Dubai International Airport
to Sheikh Zayed Road
AED60
Cappuccino
AED20
Packet of cigarettes
AED9
Daily newspaper
AED3
Bottle of champagne (duty-free only)
AED180

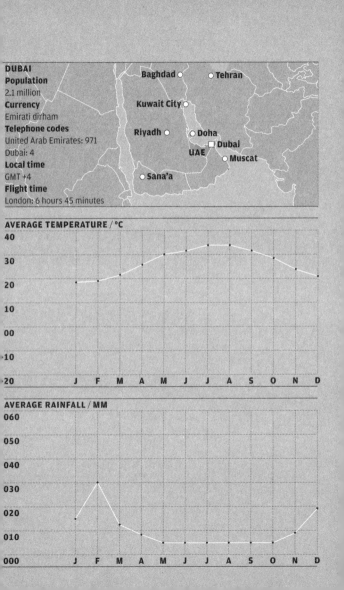

DUBAI
Population
2.1 million
Currency
Emirati dirham
Telephone codes
United Arab Emirates: 971
Dubai: 4
Local time
GMT +4
Flight time
London: 6 hours 45 minutes

Baghdad ○   ○ Tehran
Kuwait City ○
Riyadh ○   ○ Doha
       □ Dubai
UAE   ○ Muscat
Sana'a ○

AVERAGE TEMPERATURE / °C

40
30
20
10
00
-10
-20

J F M A M J J A S O N D

AVERAGE RAINFALL / MM

060
050
040
030
020
010
000

J F M A M J J A S O N D

NEIGHBOURHOODS

THE AREAS YOU NEED TO KNOW AND WHY

To help you navigate the city, we've chosen the most interesting districts (see below and the map inside the back cover) and colour-coded our featured venues, according to their location; those venues that are outside these areas are not coloured.

MARINA

Situated between Sheikh Zayed Road's shopping meccas Ibn Battuta (T 362 1900) and Mall of the Emirates (T 409 9000), and encompassing the swish Emirates Hills and Palm areas, the very vertical Marina is one of Dubai's newest districts. It's the stomping ground of the creatives from nearby Internet and Media Cities.

SHEIKH ZAYED

This sparkling strip of glass towers may not be visible from space, but it certainly dominates the skyline. Business-oriented and spotless, it is everything brave new Dubai wants to be. Its refined restaurants attract expense-account types and expats. Visit The Archive (see p033) in Safa Park.

DOWNTOWN

Fast becoming the genuine centre of a city with an excess of urban 'hearts', Downtown attracts citizens from all over Dubai. The draws are the astonishing Burj Khalifa (see p065), The Dubai Mall (T 4362 7500), the waterways of faux historical Old Town, and restaurants like La Serre (see p056).

DEIRA

Cramped, chaotic and crumbling, Deira could not be less like modern Dubai if it tried. This pedestrian paradise will finally give you a proper sense of being in the Gulf. Survey the souks, tour the city's first school (see p036) or take a ride on one of the water taxis that ply the Creek.

AL QUOZ

A dusty, industrial neighbourhood where the bulk of Dubai's manufacturing is still done, Al Quoz is the location of a blooming creative scene, and includes a number of printing and film-production companies. Many of the zone's warehouses have been transformed into art galleries, such as Ayyam (see p034) and SPM (see p078).

BUR DUBAI

The child of Dubai's 1960s building boom looks a little rough around the edges, but it is home to excellent Indian eateries and a hefty chunk of architectural heritage. Big draws are Al Fahidi Fort, the old Bastakia area and the well-restored but no longer inhabited royal residences in Shindagha.

JUMEIRAH

Dubai's premier waterfront district has a more relaxed air than elsewhere in town, with a mix of villas, cafés and malls. Chill on the pristine public beach, hang out at Comptoir 102 (see p041), and explore the side streets lined with boutiques and spas aimed at the city's deeper pockets.

CREEK

As the Creek winds towards the wildlife sanctuary of Ras Al Khor, it turns from busy waterway to urban leisure space. The ongoing Festival City development will add bars and clubs to restaurants such as Reflets (see p057) that line the river near the Golf & Yacht Club (see p070).

LANDMARKS

THE SHAPE OF THE CITY SKYLINE

For a city that has built its reputation on superlatives – the tallest tower, the most luxurious hotel – you'd expect Dubai to be awash with impressive buildings. But, in reality, when it comes to finding structures that deserve to be called landmarks, that overgrown flagpole in Jumeirah aside, the pickings are slim. At least for now.

Blame this on Dubai's twin weaknesses: its relative youth and a development plan that has always placed making money before building anything memorable. As a consequence, city planners tore down almost everything historical years ago. Of course, there are always the two towers – the sparkling Burj Khalifa (see p065) and its little sister, the Burj Al Arab (see p013) – but after a while you will suspect that their inescapable presence on T-shirts and postcards, and transmutation into incense burners, gold-plated paperweights and stuffed toys, proves Dubai's most recognisable symbols are pretty much its only recognisable symbols.

Perhaps it's best to consider the landmark question on a macro, and not a micro, level. From its beginnings as a speck on the map, a former pearl-trading town where less-interesting airlines touched down to refuel, Dubai has transformed into a sprawling, rapidly metastasising city that, shades of Ozymandias aside, views itself not just as a global hub but as *the* global hub. Forget individual buildings, Dubai's most impressive landmark may be itself.

For full addresses, see Resources.

Dubai Marina

This is the biggest manmade marina on
the planet. Naturally. At present, together
with the 40 towers of the neighbouring
Jumeirah Beach Residence, which comes
close to a Hong Kong-esque density and
constitutes the world's largest single-phase
residential development, it designates the
south-western edge of Dubai. On a clear
day, it is visible from almost 20km away
and, seen on the drive in from Abu Dhabi,
it almost suggests a city wall. It certainly
declares that you have arrived. As one of
the most desirable locations in Dubai, the
marina is also home to a few of its more
interesting structures, chief of which is
Skidmore, Owings & Merrill's Cayan Tower
(see p068), formerly known as Infinity
Tower. The 307m building, resembling
a taller and sleeker version of Santiago
Calatrava's Turning Torso in Malmö, now
dominates the marina's northern end.
Sheikh Zayed Road

Jumeirah Emirates Towers

Close to the World Trade Centre and at the entrance to Sheikh Zayed Road, two equilateral glass-and-steel triangles rise 305m and 350m into the air. One is a hotel, the other an office building; and the two are linked by Dubai's most exclusive mall, The Boulevard. Set within 170,000 sq m of landscaping that includes a waterfall and a garden, the NORR-designed towers dominate the otherwise low-rise financial district around them. The office block, which was opened in 2000, was the city's tallest finished structure for nine years. The pair have been compared to bottle openers and pencil sharpeners, but they occupy a soft spot in many locals' hearts, being among the first of Dubai's edifices to garner international attention.
Sheikh Zayed Road, T 330 0000,
www.jumeirah.com

Burj Al Arab

Okay, so WS Atkins' exterior resembles a giant Teflon beetle sitting on its haunches, and the KCA International interior is so overwrought that your initial response may be laughter, but there is still something magnificent about this hotel on first sight. Perhaps it's the way the building appears to catch the breeze when viewed from the side, or maybe it's because, at 321m, it is one of the tallest hotels in the world.

Once inside, your impression may not be as charitable. At more than 180m high, the atrium is eye-popping, but 'signature features', such as the floor-to-ceiling aquarium engulfing Al Mahara restaurant, are fairground, and the hubristic demand that you buy a coffee or souvenir just to set foot in the lobby is beyond irritating. *Jumeirah Beach Road, T 301 7777, www.jumeirah.com*

Clock Tower Roundabout
For many years, this modest roundabout
was one of the city's most prominent
landmarks. Finished in 1962, when there
were barely any paved roads to speak
of, its slender, curved brackets are meant
to evoke classical Islamic architecture.
The clock mechanism that they support
was a gift to Dubai's then ruler, Sheikh
Rashid, from his son-in-law.
Al Maktoum Road/Umm Hurair Road

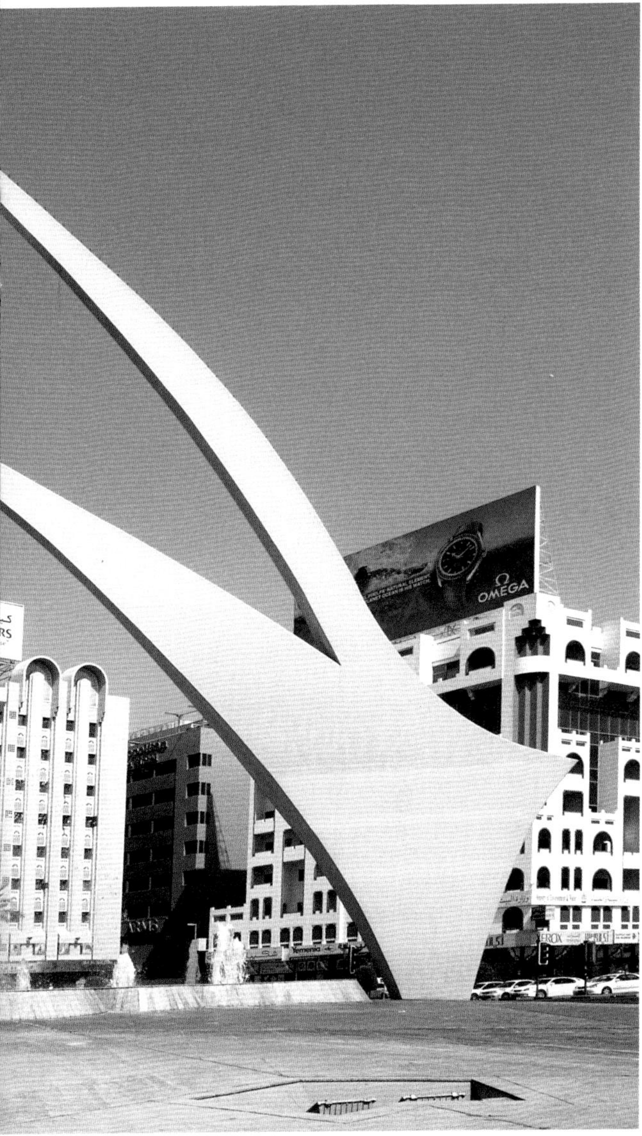
OMEGA
Yemenia

HOTELS
WHERE TO STAY AND WHICH ROOMS TO BOOK

It's rather unfortunate that Dubai's most famous hotel is also its most garish. Thankfully, the self-styled 'seven star' Burj Al Arab (see p013), aka the hotel that taste forgot, is not representative. Dubai doesn't really do budget, although some business options in Bur Dubai and Deira offer reasonable deals. The few boutique hotels, in the sense of intimate and luxurious, are XVA (opposite), the Desert Palm (see p028) and the Vida Downtown (Mohammed Bin Rashid Boulevard, T 428 6888), a reimagining of the former Qamardeen, which has been tweaked into a lovely 'little' property. Competition is fierce. All provide signature products or treatments and take pride in the warmth of their 'traditional Arab' hospitality, even if, in typical Dubai fashion, this is dispensed by Asians. The result is consistently courteous and efficient service.

During peak season, seemingly any time apart from summer, finding a room is a nightmare. Hotels feature heavily in Dubai's expansion and all its new 'cities' include a couple. The most hyped include the Anantara Dubai The Palm (East Crescent, The Palm Jumeirah, T 567 8888); the Islamicised version of Sol Kerzner's Atlantis (Crescent Road, The Palm Jumeirah, T 426 0000); and the Armani Hotel (see p018). A Palazzo Versace, replete with a chilled-sand beach, is due to open in late 2014, as is a Rosewood in the DIFC. Meanwhile, the long-delayed W may be finished by 2016. *For full addresses and room rates, see Resources.*

XVA Art Hotel

Housed in a renovated coral-stone-and-adobe home sheltered within the quiet, maze-like alleyways of the ancient traders' quarter of Bastakiya, XVA is unique. Not only does the charming property give its guests the chance to experience an upscale version of life in a Dubai that disappeared some 75 years ago, but the tasteful way the 10 rooms have been decorated with darkwood furniture, curtained bedsteads and mother-of-pearl-inlaid furnishings by Karim Rashid and Lebanese designer Nada Debs is a delight (although mind your head on the low doors). There's a gallery, a boutique and a café. The breezy rooftop terrace is a refreshing spot to unwind on steamy nights, while the courtyard (above) is the place to kick back in winter. *Al Fahidi roundabout, behind Arabian Tea House, T 353 5383, www.xvahotel.com*

Armani Hotel
Located in the Burj Khalifa (see p065), the Armani Hotel has the designer's stamp all over it, from the furniture to the spa products. Guests are treated like royalty, and the minimal interiors offer relief from the gold and gilt elsewhere in the city. Standard rooms, such as the Armani Classic (pictured), are small; the larger suites boast fantastic views.
Mohammed Bin Rashid Boulevard

The Address Downtown

Despite the self-important name, and the hotel's home in a tower whose design and twin antennae give it the appearance of a 306m-tall Dalek, The Address Downtown is sexy and knows it. The first of a chain scattered across the city, it has a style that eschews bright and brash for low-lit and sophisticated, exemplified in the lobby (opposite). It's also wired up to the nines. Embracing online services and paperless procedures, The Address has doffed its cap to the media darlings and exudes a vibe that is equal parts Silicon Valley, modern Middle East and pan-Asian chic. The Deluxe Rooms are snug, while the Premier Fountain View Rooms (above) are slightly larger, although there's only a Venetian blind separating the bed and the bathroom. Or plump for a Spa Suite; each one has a terrace with a jacuzzi.
Mohammed Bin Rashid Boulevard,
T 436 8888, www.theaddress.com

Park Hyatt

Nestled between the two halves of Dubai Creek Golf & Yacht Club (see p070), the Hyatt's whitewashed Moorish exterior, with its glistening blue cupolas, *zellige* tiles and lush tropical greenery, hints at the glamour within. The public spaces, such as the Palm and Fountain gardens, are both understated and elegant, and the light-filled guest rooms, like the Park Executive Suite (above), pitch perfect.

Open-plan bathrooms mean couples should either know one another intimately or be ready to gain that knowledge. The Terrace bar overlooking the Creek, sleek Amara spa (see p081) and wood-panelled Traiteur, one of the top French restaurants in town (it has a superb wine cellar), help make the Hyatt a one-stop destination.
Dubai Creek Golf & Yacht Club, T 602 1234, www.dubai.park.hyatt.com

Grosvenor House

From the drink and the chilled towel that greet you on arrival in the lobby (above) to the appetisers laid out in your room, the Grosvenor is a class act. The hotel is located in what, for now, feels like the edge of the city but, as more new developments are completed, Dubai's centre of gravity is shifting this way. The blue-neon exterior lighting belies the graceful interior, which has a cool Asia-meets-Middle East feel

that is carried through to the rooms. Beds big enough for a posse of bodyguards, Bulgari toiletries and sea-facing rooms overlooking the ever-rising Palm all make for a seductive package. If the in-house pools (overleaf) aren't enough, access to the beachfront pool at the Royal Méridien across the road is also available to guests. *Al Sufouh Road, Dubai Marina, T 399 8888, www.grosvenorhouse-dubai.com*

Siddharta Pool, Grosvenor House

InterContinental Festival City

The first thing you notice about this hotel is its smiling doormen, who must stand at least 2m tall. The next is the glossy lobby with rainforest-sized floral displays and crystal-studded loungers, which may be a menace to anything chiffon but sparkle enticingly in the light-filled interior. The rooms are equally polished, and the baths fill theatrically from a spout in the ceiling. Thanks to the hotel's Creek-front address, the accommodations positioned at the rear have unbroken views across the water towards the spires of Sheikh Zayed Road. For a taste of the high life, check into the Presidential Suite (above and opposite). Clean and crisp, it's favoured by the kind of guests who prefer the anonymity of in-room check-in, an adjacent crash-pad for their bodyguard, and a bathroom-with-a-vista that practically doubles as a spa. *Dubai Festival City, T 701 1111, www.intercontinental.com*

Desert Palm
Located where the city meets the sand, this hotel/resort stands in 65 hectares of land and attracts the horsey set to its stables and four polo fields. It is also a great base for desert excursions. Stay in a contemporary villa with a private garden and pool, or in the well-appointed Palm Suites (pictured). Dine at Rare.
Al Awir Road, T 323 8888,
desertpalm.peraquum.com

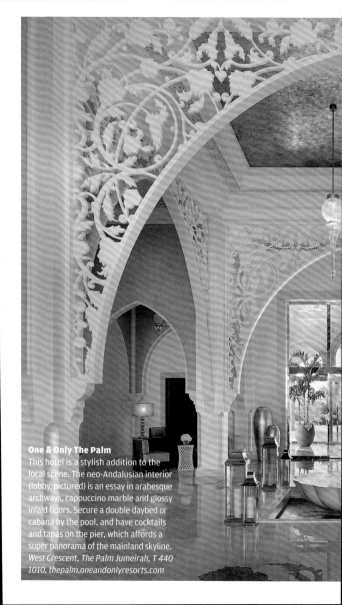

One & Only The Palm
This hotel is a stylish addition to the local scene. The neo-Andalusian interior (lobby, pictured) is an essay in arabesque archways, cappuccino marble and glossy inlaid floors. Secure a double daybed or cabana by the pool, and have cocktails and tapas on the pier, which affords a super panorama of the mainland skyline.
West Crescent, The Palm Jumeirah, T 440 1010, thepalm.oneandonlyresorts.com

24 HOURS

SEE THE BEST OF THE CITY IN JUST ONE DAY

Begin your itinerary with breakfast in the cool confines of The Archive (opposite) in verdant Safa Park, the ideal spot to watch wilting joggers and other wildlife. Then hop over to Al Quoz to tour some of Dubai's most exciting art galleries and collectives. The most notable venues are Ayyam (see p034), SPM (see p078), Carbon 12 (Unit D37, Alserkal Avenue, Street 8, T 340 6016) and J+A (Compound 5, Warehouse 15, Street 4a, T 553 950 495), which also specialises in contemporary design. At lunchtime, dive into the organic smorgasbord at the waterside branch of Baker & Spice (Marina Promenade, T 425 2240) or head Downtown for some Lebanese food at Abd El Wahab (T 423 0988) in Souk Al Bahar.

Afterwards, jump in a taxi and journey over the Creek into the narrow streets of Deira, where the restored Al Ahmadiya school (see p036) reveals what traditional Gulf architecture looked like before breeze blocks, concrete and curtain walls took over. While you are in the neighbourhood, rummage around the souks (the Gold, Deira and Spice sections are within walking distance), in search of fluorescent Syrian pants, Persian rugs from China or bars of gold bullion. Then travel back across the Creek by *abra* (water taxi) to Downtown and the panoramic sunset views from (what else?) the highest bar/restaurant on earth, At.mosphere (see p038), 122 vertiginous floors up the Burj Khalifa (see p065). *For full addresses, see Resources.*

09.30 The Archive

Embellished with more greenery than may seem likely (or sustainable) for a city that is encircled by desert, Dubai has relatively few places where it's possible to enjoy the outdoors and a good meal simultaneously. The scorching summers aren't conducive to alfresco dining, at least not before dark, but winters are a delight. This is when The Archive, an airy café/library/community space comes into its own. All glass walls and white concrete, it serves breakfast fare, snacks and salads. If the sight of breathless joggers (even in winter, Dubai can get toasty) and surprisingly sprightly suitcase-sized birds don't capture your attention, the rows of smartly displayed tomes (from treatises on Islamic textiles to children's books in Arabic) surely will. *Gate 5, Safa Park, T 349 4033, www.thearchive.ae*

11.00 Ayyam

An outpost of the Damascus gallery, Ayyam Al Quoz, which has a second Dubai branch (T 439 2395) in the DIFC, is charged with bringing contemporary Syrian art to the world. As undertakings go, this one's vital. Syria produces some of the region's most sophisticated art, and its ongoing civil war makes Ayyam a lifeline. Located in Dubai's expanding art quarter, a 'warehouse' zone with fewer actual industries every year, Ayyam shows excellent Arab (and Iranian) art. It's a spacious and cool white venue, but it is the power of its featured artists, such as Syria's Ammar al-Beik, Tammam Azzam and Abdul Karim Majdal al-Beik; Palestine's Samia Halaby; and Lebanon's Walid al-Masri, Khaled Takreti and Nadim Karam ('99 Objects Possible to Find on a Cloud', left), that creates the atmosphere. *Warehouse B11, Alserkal Avenue, Street 8, T 323 6242, www.ayyamgallery.com*

15.00 Al Ahmadiya

Until the 1950s, Dubai was a big village divided into three districts: Shindagha, Bastakiya and Deira. Now swallowed by expansion, Deira's Al Ras remains a good locale to view how Dubai looked before it discovered oil. The mishmash of old and new, decaying low-rises and towers, is home to a few spartan but beautiful coral-stone and gypsum merchant houses. Al Ahmadiya, Dubai's first school, was built by a pearl trader in 1912. The two-storey building set around a sandy courtyard has thick walls, reed ceilings, decorative arches and plaques inscribed with Koranic verses. In places, shells and other animal life are embedded in the coral. Although closed in 1963, the school was saved in 2000 and, along with the pearl trader's house behind it, is now a museum. Closed Saturdays.
Al Ras, T 226 0286

19.00 At.mosphere Burj Khalifa
Adam Tihany's interior may smack of an
oversized, luxuriously done-out humidor,
and prices can be stratospheric, but this
lounge/restaurant's elevated vibe is a
Dubai highlight. Perched 422m above
ground, it's curiously difficult to get a
sensation of height. The awesome vista
is most magnificent after dark, when the
city takes on a beauty it lacks by day.
Level 122, Burj Khalifa, T 888 3444

URBAN LIFE

CAFÉS, RESTAURANTS, BARS AND NIGHTCLUBS

Nightlife in Dubai is expat-oriented. Comedy venues feature acts fresh from London, and dance clubs host DJs who were in Istanbul the night before and will be in Barcelona the next. It's all a bit, well, blah. Because alcohol is served only at (five-star) hotels – although two venues in Jumeirah Emirates Towers, The Ivy (T 319 8767) and The Agency (T 319 8780), bend that rule slightly – nightlife often (partly) revolves around them. To escape the 'great indoors' and still enjoy a drink, head to the seaside Nasimi Beach (Atlantis, Crescent Road, The Palm Jumeirah, T 4426 2626).

When it comes to eating out, the city is more diverse. Dubai is packed with franchises by multi-starred chefs (if that's your thing), but the more interesting options are located in the less-manicured neighbourhoods. If you're not fussed about alcohol (or interiors), Abshar (Jumeirah Beach Road, T 394 0950) has cracking Iranian food, whereas Samad Al Iraqi (Jumeirah Beach Road, T 342 7887) can't be beat for Iraqi treats such as *masgoof*. Feast on cheap-as-chips Pakistani dishes at Ravi Restaurant (Al Satwa Road, T 331 5353) and explore Deira and Karama for no-frills eateries. Top-notch Emirati cuisine is difficult to find, so if you fancy some *dango* or *ouzi*, you'll have to hit the tourist traps. Try Local House (51 Al Bastakiya, T 354 0705) or the dancing-camels-with-buffet blowout at Al Hadheerah (Bab Al Shams Desert Resort & Spa, T 4809 6194). *For full addresses, see Resources.*

Comptoir 102

Tucked in an old villa, Comptoir 102 may not look like much from the outside, but inside it's a different story. Packed with character and well thought-out, it's a nifty mix of boutique and restaurant. The main problem your visit will present is deciding whether to eat before or after you shop. To that end, you can browse a range of sophisticated designer goodies (artwork, objects, furniture and fashion), mostly French but with numerous regional finds thrown in. Run by a trio of design-literate expat women, everything, from the menu to the merchandise, is decided collectively. The food is fresh and local (not easy in the Emirates) and, where possible, organic. Raw, vegan, gluten-free, dairy-free and sugar-free options are also available.

102 Jumeirah Beach Road, T 385 4555, www.comptoir102.com

Pierchic

Perched at the end of a pier, this dark, fortress-like place with its curious little wind towers looks rather gothic. The walkway can seem endless, but once you arrive, the laidback bar and magnificent view of the sea and Burj Al Arab (see p013) make up for the exertion, especially after a premium Kir Royale. Pierchic is also a restaurant and, as befits its location, the menu is mostly seafood. The prices are steep, especially since the portions tend towards the *nouvelle*, although the high quality of the ingredients is evident in every bite. However, the real pleasures to be had here are of the liquid kind. So order a cocktail, settle down on a sofa lounger out on the deck and wait for one of Dubai's stunning sunsets.
Madinat Jumeirah Resort, T 366 6730, www.jumeirah.com

MAKE Business Hub

A response to Dubai's burgeoning creative community and dearth of affordable and/ or desirable workspace, MAKE is among the best of a crop of communal office zones that combine ultrafast internet access and other services with food and even a little fun. There are a variety of seating options, from single tables to loveseats and cabins. Aesthetically, the vibe is industrial-lite: bare concrete, blondwood and exposed ducting. Sessions run from an hour to all day, and enclosed glass booths for large meetings or privacy mean this is the ideal alternative to doing business in a hotel lobby or a rented office. Also good for a casual chat, or coffee while you surf the interweb, this branch is the first of many. *Al Fattan Tower, Al Sufouh Road, Jumeirah Beach Residences, T 392 9216, www.makebusinesshub.com*

THE One

Best described as a cross between Pier 1 and The Conran Shop, this formerly fey café, now robustly butched-up, is popular with male interior decorators and their female friends. About as close as Dubai gets to a gay café, you half expect the slender Filipino waitpersons to call each other 'honey'. They don't. Not in public, at least. The menu is fabulous too – carrot and coriander soup, lamb tagine, onion, asparagus and gruyère panini, and more varieties of tea than you believe could exist. Survey the clientele, who are most certainly surveying you, or else enjoy the view of the imposing neo-Fatimid style Jumeirah Mosque next door, as you decide which of the eight inventive cheesecakes you'll be partaking of today.
Jumeirah Beach Road, T 345 6687, www.theone.com

Okku

Don't let Okku's beautiful crowd of see-and-be-seensters put you off. Most of them make for the private dining areas upstairs. And don't allow the jellyfish tanks, DJ booth and pulsing fibre-optic wall to mislead you into thinking that Okku is anything other than a restaurant, because the food, such as yellowfin tuna carpaccio in a ponzu sauce, is terrific.
The H, 1 Sheikh Zayed Road, T 501 8777

The Farm

On the dusty fringes of town, where only those optimistic enough to have made the International Academic City home would frequent, a vision in green has sprung up. Comprising more than 6km of canals and swathes of parkland, the development that is the Zaal family's Al Barari Villas rises from its stony surroundings. At its heart is The Farm, a café/restaurant ostensibly for residents, but actually open to anyone.

The healthy, fusion-influenced global menu includes the kinds of ingredients you'd find at a vegetarian love-fest. Meat-eaters are not forgotten, though, and some dishes can be tailored to requirements. Come for a morning yoga session, then lunch in one of the hotel-chic glass pavilions floating above the edges of a small, bird-filled lake. *Al Barari, opposite Falcon City, T 392 5660, www.thefarmdubai.com*

Indego

You may eat in the company of Hindu gods and other tchotchkes, but the interior at Indego is sufficiently uncluttered to leave the focus on the food. Devised by Vineet Bhatia, of London's Michelin-starred Rasoi, it still serves the best contemporary Indian food in Dubai a decade or so after opening. The menu is traditional with a few twists, such as ingredients like rose petals, vanilla beans, truffle oil and morel mushrooms.

Some dishes are more successful than others, but they all deserve to be sampled. The pot-roasted ginger lamb chops alone justify a visit, and the *methi malai paneer*, a cheese flavoured with fenugreek and stuffed with mango chutney, and pan-seared scallops, an adventurous mingling of spices and textures, are toothsome.
*Grosvenor House, Al Sufouh Road,
T 317 6000, www.indegobyvineet.com*

MusicHall

Imported from Beirut, where owner Michel Elefteriades has been making the best-clad booties shake for a decade, MusicHall has all the theatricality of its older sister. With red velvet, and plush seating and curtains, the venue is visually out of the 1890s, but even if the 'dinner and show' concept has been around since the Victorians, neither the meal nor the entertainment here are sedate. Known for his love of tango, reggae and Balkan gypsy madness, Elefteriades, the self-styled Emperor of Nowhereistan (his unilaterally declared dominion has a flag), likes to mix things up – think classic Arab chanson set to *son cubano*. Although Dubai's clubbers haven't copied Lebanon's, who dance on the tables, rest assured that they know how to make some noise.
Jumeirah Zabeel Saray, West Crescent, The Palm, T 270 8670, www.themusichall.com

The Pantry

Publicly setting the bar high for itself, a Dubai proclivity, this café/deli in a rather unassuming building aims to be 'the place for breakfast, lunch, dinner and all meals in-between'. Presumption aside, it is a local gem and, although its look is more noughties than now, in terms of its ethics, support of artisan producers, pursuit of the organic and 'we are family' ambience, it is both old-timey and contemporary.

The flavours are decidedly 'international deli', and despite a few upmarket surprises, such as the truffled lobster risotto, the feeling is more comfort than cosmopolitan. Most of the ingredients used to create the menu, as well as some choice ready-made preparations, are available to buy, so you can take a piece of the Pantry home.
Wasl Square, Al Hadeeqa Street,
T 388 3868, www.pantrycafe.me

La Serre

Prior to La Serre, if you fancied something French, your destination would have been the local La Petite Maison. Although still popular, especially at lunch, the bistro is now challenged by this greenhouse-like box wrapped around the front of the Vida hotel. Bishop Design's white, mirror-clad interior may say Cannes 1982, but Izu Ani's menu is a modern, seasonally observant set of sumptuous Mediterranean dishes and French classics, with an edge. The service feels almost invisible. You will not be 'persuaded' of the merits of your choice, but your waiter will have plenty of answers to your menu questions. Packed and occasionally raucous at night, thanks to the open kitchen and buzzing bar, La Serre is a simple, sexy and succulent joy. *Mohammed Bin Rashid Boulevard, T 428 6969, www.laserre.ae*

Reflets par Pierre Gagnaire

Stylistically somewhere between a boudoir and a brasserie (or even a bordello – the bathrooms are nothing short of theatrical), French chef Pierre Gagnaire's restaurant is a winner. The dishes are exquisitely presented works of art, interpreted here by Olivier Bile, and the emphasis is on all things fresh or, rather, freshly flown in; with the exception of locally caught fish, the ingredients come from elsewhere. The cuisine is characterised by the type of taste and texture combinations that are best described as 'multisensory hits', and hints at molecular gastronomy without ever straying into its more recherché territory. As it's hoped diners will sample a number of courses, portions here are designed to titillate not to sate.
InterContinental Festival City, T 701 1111, www.ichotelsgroup.com/intercontinental

The Roof Top

The view is less attractive now that The Palm occupies half the horizon, but this venue is as seductive as ever. The chillout soundtrack and cushion-strewn divans combine to create a serene atmosphere. Play pasha for a day. Slip off your shoes, order a cocktail and a couple of plates of mezze, and forget that the world exists.
One&Only Royal Mirage, Al Sufouh Road, T 399 9999, www.oneandonlyresorts.com

Zuma

For its aesthetic impact alone, Zuma still impresses. The Japanese cuisine franchise occupies a double-height space in Dubai's financial district, the right location given the average price of a meal. Pull up a seat at the sushi counter, opt for a more formal setting in the lower-floor dining area, or spend an evening in the loungey space upstairs (right), which has a striking bar decked out with antique wood and backlit sake bottles. The signature dishes include crispy fried squid with a tangy green-chilli-and-lime dressing, and miso-marinated black cod in hoba leaf. By day, Zuma draws the kind of clientele often seen in the Square Mile, and if by night all the jackets and ties disappear, conversations about barefoot pilgrims and bottom fishers reveal that this is still a trader crowd.
Gate Village 6, Trade Centre 2, DIFC,
T 425 5660, www.zumarestaurant.com

INSIDER'S GUIDE

TIMA OUZDEN, DESIGNER

Born in the northern Caucasus, Tima Ouzden has lived in Dubai for the past 17 years. She has a background in marketing, business planning and fashion design, and currently alternates between designer and cultural producer, a combination that means she's done everything from creating dresses to curating art shows.

When it comes to buying other people's clothes, Ouzden visits IF Boutique (26 Umm Al Sheif Road, T 394 7260), the local branch of the Lebanese concept store, for its labels such as Comme des Garçons, AF Vandevorst, Ann Demeulemeester, Ivan Grundahl and Yohji Yamamoto, plus accessories and perfumes from Olfactive Studio. Art, too, features prominently in her life, and in addition to A4 (Alserkal Avenue), an alternative arts/community hub in Al Quoz, she likes Grey Noise (Unit 24, Alserkal Avenue, Street 8, T 416 1900), a contemporary gallery specialising in experimental work from South Asia, the Middle East and Europe.

Evenings? For a quiet start, Ouzden has dinner at Cucina (JW Marriott, Abu Baker Al Siddique Road, T 607 7977), famous for its ice-cream 'spaghetti' made at the table in a mincer and served on a raspberry coulis. Come the weekend, it's dancing to after-dark beats courtesy of Nasrawi and Mehdi Ansari at the Analog Room (The Q Underground, Holiday Inn Al Barsha, T 508 833 172) – a weekly subterranean electronic music night held every Thursday. *For full addresses, see Resources.*

ARCHITOUR

A GUIDE TO DUBAI'S ICONIC BUILDINGS

Dubai apparently still believes that by calling every new building 'iconic', however undeservedly, it will become so. Two decades ago, you could get away with such silliness. In architectural terms, the majority of the Gulf was low-rise, so if you threw up a tall building, you could claim the cutting edge. That is no longer the case. Flush from the last oil boom, Dubai's neighbours have also decided their cachet should, in part, rest upon starchitecture, so the heat is on.

Dubai has a lot of skyscrapers. Few do more than remind you of better ones elsewhere. Most make you wish that they hadn't been built. Some ambitious projects of the pre-Crash years – The World, Dynamic Architecture's Rotating Tower and Zaha Hadid's opera house, for example – are either toast or have stalled. Developers Emaar unveiled plans in 2012 for a 'multipurpose' opera house as part of their new Downtown Culture District, and Rem Koolhaas' Waterfront has been bowdlerised. However, SOM's elegant Cayan Tower (see p068) and Foster + Partners' Index (see p069) are up.

The criticism that followed Dubai's precipitous plummet from financial grace appears to have been chastening, so it could be that in future the city will embrace quality over quantity. If not, in a decade or so, when its neighbours come into their own, Dubai's star will wane. And if there were anything the city that hype built could not bear, it would be to surrender the limelight to its sisters. *For full addresses, see Resources.*

Burj Khalifa

From its wide base, this Y-shaped tower, which was designed by SOM with Adrian Smith, spirals upwards, sections falling away, until its slim central core emerges in the top few hundred metres. Opened in January 2010, the world's tallest building is a mixed-use tower that soars 828m into Dubai's dusty sky. Its shape is based on the geometry of a desert flower, but the impression of Gotham on Viagra is far too potent to miss. Islamic motifs are also alluded to, albeit in a largely symbolic manner, and technical tricks include a double-glass skin and lift that whooshes up to the 124th-floor observation deck in 60 seconds. The Armani Hotel (see p018) occupies six floors, and bar/restaurant At.mosphere (see p038) sits on level 122.
1 Emaar Boulevard, T 888 8124,
www.burjkhalifa.ae

The Gate
Yes, you have seen something similar
before – in Paris. Got it yet? No? Well
then, picture a cartouche of romantic
neoclassical sculpture on either column,
replace the square arch with a round
one, and you could almost be on the
Champs-Élysées. The portal to Dubai's
business hub is proof that tasteful
reinterpretation is not a bad thing.
DIFC, Sheikh Zayed Road, www.difc.ae

Cayan Tower

Begun in 2006 as the Infinity Tower, this structure rises above the seaward entry to Dubai Marina (see p010) in an arrested helix that twists towards, well, infinity. Delayed by the economic downturn and a series of construction difficulties, such as the foundations flooding when the seawall was breached in 2007, it finally opened in 2013. Although it isn't the first twisting tower – Malmö pipped Dubai to that post in 2001 with Santiago Calatrava's Turning Torso – it is the highest. And possibly the most graceful. Cayan's sharp and stylish shape results from each floorplate being rotated by 1.2 degrees. Expressed over a height of 307m, this seemingly negligible rotation results in a full 90-degree turn, permitting fortunate residents views of both the Marina and the Arabian Gulf. *Dubai Marina, Plot 10b, www.cayan.net*

The Index

Norman Foster's prominent 80-storey erection hulks over the still-emerging neighbourhood opposite the sprawling Dubai Mall. Austere in its slab-like form, it resembles a supersized monolith and a slender version of the Tyrell Corporation headquarters in *Blade Runner*, and exudes a retro-futuristic chic. Finished in 2010, the mixed-use office and residential tower the two functions are separated by a double-height sky lobby) is orientated along an east-west axis to enable the twin concrete cores to minimise heat gain, while solar shades on the south facade further lessen the sun's impact. As such, it is not only one of Dubai's most pleasing buildings (and few real pieces of architecture), it's also environmentally laudable, requiring substantially less electricity to keep cool. *312 Road, www.up.ae/index*

Dubai Creek Golf & Yacht Club
This club is not only conveniently located, a golf course smack in the middle of town between the business district of Garhoud and the Creek itself, but its clubhouse is also one of the most distinctive buildings in Dubai. It opened in 1993, designed by UK firm Godwin Austen Johnson, known for championing a modern Arabian style at hotels such as One&Only and Bab Al Shams. The sharply curving planes that intersect above the glass atrium are pure futurism, and pay homage to the sailing boats that formerly dominated the Creek. The clubhouse has the essence of a Middle Eastern take on the Sydney Opera House, but most visitors probably don't notice, and are attracted instead by an 18-hole, par-71 championship-standard course, not to mention a floodlit nine-hole alternative that can be played on until 10pm.
Al Garhoud Road, T 295 6000,
www.dubaigolf.com

SHOPPING

THE BEST RETAIL THERAPY AND WHAT TO BUY

Consumerism is a national sport in Dubai, and when temperatures often exceed 40°C, who'd want to be kicking a football around? It has the best shopping in the Gulf, and the sheer number of brands (tax-free but not cheap) explains its appeal to visitors from India, Iran and Russia. For others, it's less tempting. In a city where most things come from somewhere else, there isn't much that your average Londoner, Singaporean or Tokyoite couldn't find at home.

But it isn't all bad. On the edible side of things, there's now a Friday morning organic market (www.ripeme.com) in Safa Park. The souks are fun and, although they lack the gravitas of those in Aleppo (sadly, now in ruins) and Shiraz, are atmospheric. Dubai is low on its own boutiques and small businesses, but it's a young city and local designers are popping up. In The Dubai Mall, check out Madiyah Al Sharqi's line and the shoes of Camilla Skovgaard, both stocked at Symphony (T 330 8050), and Tahir Sultan's slinky creations, which are sometimes sold at Sauce (T 339 9696).

What Dubai does offer is custom-made goods. Bring a photo of what you want, pick up some material at the Textiles Souk (off Al Fahidi Street) and haggle at tailors such as Kachins (Cosmos Lane, Meena Bazaar, T 352 1386) or Dream Girl (Al Fahidi Street, T 352 1841). For jewellery, try the Gold Souk (Old Baladiya Street) or the upscale Gold & Diamond Park (Sheikh Zayed Road, T 362 7777). *For full addresses, see Resources.*

O' de Rose

This wonderland of domestic wares is mostly dedicated to home furnishings. O' de Rose stocks a small but colourful collection of everything from carpets, sofas and throws to tables, knick-knacks and artwork, with some clothing thrown into the mix. The collection is envisaged as a showcase for Middle Eastern and Central Asian goods, and embraces both the contemporary and the traditional.

The midcentury furniture reupholstered in antique fabrics, the brassware, and the tables inlaid with mother-of-pearl are the work of Lebanese designers Bokja, Karen Chekerdjian and Nada Debs, respectively. There are also enough Syrian mirrors, Iranian tiles and Tunisian tableware to keep you in orientalist heaven.
999 Al Wasl Road, Umm Suqeim 2,
T 348 7990, www.o-derose.com

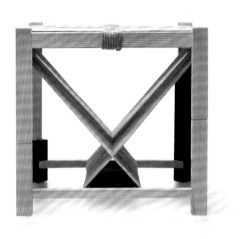

Kasa

After seven years working in marketing, Khalid Shafar decided to do something creative. The result is an ongoing series of furniture and objects that, unusually in the 'city that depends on others', are actually designed by their maker, who trained in London and New Zealand, and is more than capable of turning his ideas into reality. This sets him apart from the local design pack, but the fact that he is also Emirati makes him a rarity. His work, like the 'Illusion Stool' (above), AED5,500, made from ash and Danish rope, is a mix of the whimsical and the modernist, and his polished-concrete showroom in Ras al Khor, Kasa, is a refreshing change from the self-conscious Arabianism that passes elsewhere for contemporary design. *Community 612, Street 22a, Ras Al Khor Industrial 1, www.khalidshafar.com*

Boutique 1

Admittedly, on entering this boutique you will probably ponder why this sandy city is so obsessed with the all-white interior, but the array of clothes here is excellent. Aside from a handful of notable regional exceptions (the Dubai-based Kage springs to mind), these are not labels that will be new to you, and it isn't as though most of the brands in Dubai don't have dedicated boutiques elsewhere in the city. However, the care with which the range is selected takes almost all of the guesswork out of assembling your wardrobe. The temptation to walk in and order one of everything (and as this is the Gulf, it's entirely possible this does happen) may be overwhelming, but it's worth your while to have a good look around. You may just find yourself a lovely little surprise to take back home.
The Walk at Jumeirah Beach Residence,
T 425 7888, www.boutique1.com

SPM

SPM's interest in European/world art isn't the only thing setting it aside from the rest of the Dubai art pack, whose main mission is the promotion and sale of regional work. A gallery it may be, but it also doubles as a collector's lounge and a community art space and is, in effect, the region's first private museum open to the public. The creation of Ramin Salsali, SPM combines displays of the Iranian's own art collection, much of which is contemporary and from Iran, with shows organised by in-house director Figen Keil (above are works by Nazzy Beglari, Terry O'Neill, Abed Bibi and Michel Haddi). Although Salsali lives between Hamburg and Dubai, he is often on the premises and, together with Keil, happy to offer advice to aspiring collectors. *Unit 14, Alserkal Avenue, Street 8, T 380 9600, www.salsalipm.com*

SPORTS AND SPAS

WORK OUT, CHILL OUT OR JUST WATCH

Doha may have pipped Dubai to the post by creating a national sporting academy (Aspire), to train the Arab athletes of the future, but Dubai is no quitter, and hopes are high that it will make up the lost ground when the long-awaited and the even longer-delayed multibillion-dollar Sports City (Sheikh Mohammed Bin Zayed Road, T 425 1111) is finished. When that will be is uncertain. Parts of the development, including a world-class cricket stadium, are open, but the training academies are yet to see the light of day.

When it comes to armchair athletics, though, Dubai does have the market covered. In the winter season, when temperatures are more palatable, there is one global sporting event after another. In addition to homegrown pleasures such as the frequent camel races, highlights include the Dubai Rugby Sevens international tournament in November (www.dubairugby7s.com), the Dubai Tennis Championship and Dubai Tour professional cycling race in February, and the Dubai Desert Classic and Dubai World Cup (see p084) horse-racing events during the first quarter of the year.

Those who are determined to participate can take aim with the Dubai Archers (Sharjah Wanderers Golf Club, T 6558 6239), go scuba-diving with Al Boom Diving (Al Wasi Road, T 342 2993) or Scubatec (Shop 15, Karama Sana Building, T 334 8988), or whoosh down the 400m run at Ski Dubai (see p086).

For full addresses, see Resources.

Amara

A full treatment session at the luxurious Amara spa in the Park Hyatt (see p022) is a serious business. Start with a foot and hand wash, followed by a mineral salt body scrub for 45 minutes, then rinse off in the outdoor rain shower in your private courtyard. Relax in the garden with some tea, dried apricots and almonds, before returning for an hour-long aromatherapy treatment or Swedish massage, during which you'll be alternately pounded and slathered with oils that will leave your skin soft for days. Return to the shower, then pull up a lounger in the central courtyard where, come the evening, the oil lights in the pool and the star-filled desert sky will relieve any residual tension. Prepare to leave remade and ready to fall into bed. *Park Hyatt, Al Garhoud Road, T 602 1660, www.dubai.park.hyatt.com*

Spa at The Address Downtown

Dubai isn't short of five-star spas, many staffed by nimble-fingered South-East Asians who are trained to massage even the most stubborn muscles into blissful acquiescence. The Address' three-hour-long signature treatment, Restore and Hydrate, places you in the perfect state to bask in the post-pamper panoramic views of the Burj Khalifa (see p065), The Dubai Mall and the faux crenellations of Old Town. But the real reason to come here is the hotel's five-tiered pool, to which spa-goers have access. It never feels crowded and is built in such a way that sinking to eye level in the lowest pool leaves you with only the Dubai Fountain and the base of the world's tallest tower for company.
Mohammed Bin Rashid Boulevard, T 436 8755, www.theaddress.com

Meydan Racecourse

It goes without saying that the Dubai government's 60,000-seat racetrack is the largest in the world. Less expected were the 12 non-stop hours of live local TV coverage it enjoyed when it opened in early 2010. Still, it's an impressive creation, equipped with both turf and Tapeta tracks. The equestrian season is capped by the Dubai World Cup, the horse race with the world's highest prize purse. Meydan's ambitions don't end there. The complex also encompasses a five-star hotel, an IMAX cinema and slew of fine-dining restaurants. When the whole development is complete, its facilities will include a golf course, marina, museum, stables, residential quarter and, of course, plenty of shops. *Al Meydan Road, Nad Al Sheba, T 327 0000, www.meydan.ae*

Ski Dubai

A trip to Dubai, the self-styled Las Vegas of the Middle East, wouldn't be complete without indulging in at least one tacky experience. So remind yourself you're in one of the world's most surreal cities and head for the five indoor slopes at Ski Dubai. Late evenings are best if you want to avoid first-timers (open until 11pm, Sunday to Wednesday; 12am, Thursday to Friday). *Mall of the Emirates, Sheikh Zayed Road, T 409 4000, www.skidxb.com*

ESCAPES

WHERE TO GO IF YOU WANT TO LEAVE TOWN

So much conspicuous consumption eventually wearies even the most ardent capitalist. When thoughts turn to escape, Dubai offers four options: the desert, the sea, another emirate or a flight out. As for neighbouring cities, it's only in terms of development and amenities that the six other emirates differ. That said, a trip to the capital, Abu Dhabi (see p093), which has expansion plans that make Dubai look like a test run, Ras Al Khaimah (see p100) or Sharjah (see p102) will give a sharper sense of regional context. The alternatives include Isfahan (see p096), or Kish, Iran's kooky island of relative decadence off its southern coast. Or venture across to see the museums and other contemporary architectural additions in Bahrain's historic Al Muharraq district, which is fast becoming the Gulf's most interesting arts quarter.

In winter, the desert has many draws. There are hot springs at Ain Al Ghamour (rough and ready, not Zumthor-esque), ancient villages (Hatta), historic forts (Al Bithnah), archaeological sites (Wadi Al Hayl), and dune-bashing (www.desertsafaridubai.com). A word of warning, though. Unless you're a connoisseur of kitsch, pass on packages that combine an afternoon of adrenaline with visits to Bedouin 'encampments', henna tattoo sessions or belly dancing. For more edifying pursuits, try the wildlife-strewn island of Sir Bani Yas, which now boasts a luxury resort (see p092). *For full addresses, see Resources.*

Museum of Islamic Art, Doha, Qatar

Doha is hardly short of stunning modern architecture, it's just that nearly all of it is located within the campus of the Qatar Foundation and casual tours are, sadly, not possible. Thankfully, IM Pei's blockily beautiful Museum of Islamic Art, opened in 2008, single-handedly makes a trip to Doha worthwhile. Rising 60m above the seaside corniche, this austere white meditation on geometric shapes, a dome that becomes an octagon that becomes squares that become triangles, is, without question, of today, but also references the past. Jean-Michel Wilmotte's minimalist interiors (above) are a showcase for one of the world's best collections of Islamic art, from calligraphy to ceramics. Daily flights from Dubai take about an hour. *Al Corniche, T +974 422 4446, www.mia.org.qa*

Museum of Islamic Art, Doha, Qatar

Anantara All Yamm Villa Resort

Imagine you were an emir, owned more islands than you needed and had a passion for wildlife. What would you do? Enter Abu Dhabi's Sir Bani Yas island, which until the 1990s was a private reserve belonging to HH Sheikh Zayed, founding father of the UAE. Home to oryx and cheetahs, giraffes and hyenas, and myriad birds, it now hosts the occasional human too, at Anantara's All Yamm Villa Resort. The hotel's main draw is its string of villas (above) dotted along the coral beach and among the mangroves. Based on *barasti*, the palm-frond huts once found across the region, they are simple and secluded, and come, as one would expect from one of Asia's premier purveyors of spa-centred luxury, with all the mods but no cons.

Sir Bani Yas, Abu Dhabi, T 2801 4200, www.al-yamm.anantara.com

Abu Dhabi

The largest of the seven emirates that make up the UAE, Abu Dhabi is not only the country's capital and centre of political power, it is also its richest city, floating on a sea of oil that resource-strapped Dubai can only envy. Smaller and less glitzy than its more famous sister, Abu Dhabi retains traces of the modest fishing port it was when oil was first discovered in 1958. But not for long. The city is positioning itself as the region's cultural epicentre, with better-funded arts festivals and a host of mega-museums. Rising on Saadiyat Island are Jean Nouvel's Louvre (due to open in 2015) and Gehry's Guggenheim (2017). Elsewhere, the state's bold ambitions are visible in the form of edgy buildings such as the Yas Viceroy hotel (T 2656 0000), which has a top-flight ESPA spa (above), and straddles an F1 racetrack (overleaf).

Isfahan, Iran

An hour's flight from Dubai (Iran Air flies twice a week), Isfahan is Iran's equivalent of Rome or Athens. The beloved city of the Safavid emperors and twice the capital of Persia, it feels like a massive open-air museum. It's hard to know where to start. How about Naghsh-e Jahan square (so large it's nicknamed Nesf-e Jahan or 'half of the world'), flanked by the frescoed 17th-century Ali Qapu Palace and Sheikh Lotfallah Mosque, with its breathtaking mosaicked dome? Or the remarkable Imam Mosque (opposite), or 11th-century Friday Mosque (above)? Or the restored Ali Gholi Agha Alley bathhouse, the Hasht Behesht palace, or the Armenian churches of Vank? Perhaps something older? If so, the ancient capital of Persepolis and the rock-cut tombs of Naqsh-e Rustam are only a one-hour drive up the road.

Liwa Oasis

Arrive in the UAE expecting *The English Patient*-style vistas and you may feel let down. The desert is vast, but rarely feels remote. The oasis town of Liwa may not seem so either, but drive further out and you'll arrive on the fringes of the Empty Quarter, a huge sea of sand stretching across Arabia. Stay at the Qasr Al Sarab Desert Resort (pictured; T 2886 2088) for some five-star pampering.

Banyan Tree Al Wadi, Ras Al Khaimah
Set amid the sand dunes and ghaf trees of a private nature reserve in the Wadi Khadeja, Banyan Tree's first Middle Eastern property blends Asian styling and Islamic motifs to create a contemporary Arabian aesthetic. Eschewing pseudo-historicism and overblown Bedouinisms, the resort is a combination of tents and villas, such as the Al Rimal Deluxe Pool villa (above), laid out to maximise views but maintain privacy. Many of the individual pools, for example, are shielded from one another by sand dunes. A signature restaurant overlooks a watering hole and a series of watchtowers spans the 100-hectare site, so guests are assured that, should their fellow lodgers fail to interest them, there is plenty more wildlife to observe. *Al Mazraa, T 7206 7777, www.banyantree.com*

Sharjah

The emirate of Sharjah doesn't look a bit like its bigger sister. Admittedly, your first sight is a shopping mall, but soon you will notice that the high-rises aren't as high, the hotels haven't as many stars and the restaurants are a sober affair. There is an emphasis on Islamic practices (alcohol, nightclubs, short sleeves and miniskirts are prohibited), Arabic dominates, and, in place of glossy malls, there are museums and traditional bazaars. Prohibition, family values — you may be wondering why you would visit? Although Sharjah may be too sedate to live in, it is home to the majority of museums in the UAE. Those devoted to art (T 6568 8222), archaeology (T 6566 5466) and Islamic civilisation (T 6565 5455) are all of interest. It's also home to the Gulf's edgiest arts festival, the Sharjah Biennale (www.sharjahbiennial.org).

NOTES
SKETCHES AND MEMOS

RESOURCES

CITY GUIDE DIRECTORY

HOTELS

ADDRESSES AND ROOM RATES

The Address Downtown 020
Room rates:
double, from AED1,600;
Deluxe Room, from AED1,600;
Premier Fountain View, from AED2,520;
Spa Suite, from AED3,700
Sheikh Mohammed Bin Rashid Boulevard
T 436 8888
www.theaddress.com

Anantara All Yamm Villa Resort 092
Room rates:
double, from AED1,570;
villa, AED2,200
Sir Bani Yas
Abu Dhabi
T 2801 4200
www.al-yamm.anantara.com

Anantara Dubai The Palm 016
Room rates:
double, from AED1,850
East Crescent
The Palm Jumeirah
T 567 8888
www.anantara.com

Armani Hotel 018
Room rates:
double, from AED4,200;
Armani Classic, AED4,400
Sheikh Mohammed Bin Rashid Boulevard
T 888 3888
www.armanihotels.com

Atlantis 016
Room rates:
double, from AED1,075
Crescent Road
The Palm Jumeirah
T 426 0000
www.atlantisthepalm.com

Banyan Tree Al Wadi 100
Room rates:
double, from AED2,350;
Al Rimal Deluxe Pool Villa, AED2,350
Al Mazraa
Ras Al Khaimah
T 7206 7777
www.banyantree.com

Desert Palm 028
Room rates:
double, from AED1,050;
Palm Suite, from AED1,255;
Pool Villa, from AED3,550
Al Awir Road
T 323 8888
desertpalm.peraquum.com

Grosvenor House 023
Room rates:
double, from AED2,500
Al Sufouh Road
Dubai Marina
T 399 8888
www.grosvenorhouse-dubai.com

InterContinental Festival City 026
Room rates:
double, from AED900;
Presidential Suite, from AED3,900
Dubai Festival City
T 701 1111
www.intercontinental.com

One & Only The Palm 030
Room rates:
double, from AED1,000
West Crescent
The Palm Jumeirah
T 440 1010
thepalm.oneandonlyresorts.com

Park Hyatt 022
  Room rates:
  double, from AED780;
  Park Executive Suite, from AED3,195
  Dubai Creek Golf & Yacht Club
  Al Garhoud Road
  T 602 1234
  www.dubai.park.hyatt.com
Qasr Al Sarab Desert Resort 098
  Room rates:
  double, from AED1,450
  1 Qasr Al Sarab Road
  Abu Dhabi
  T 2886 2088
  www.qasralsarab.anantara.com
Vida Downtown 016
  Room rates:
  double, from AED2,200
  Sheikh Mohammed Bin Rashid Boulevard
  T 428 6888
  www.vida-hotels.com
XVA Art Hotel 017
  Room rates:
  double, from AED800
  Al Fahidi roundabout
  Behind Arabian Tea House
  T 353 5383
  www.xvahotel.com
Yas Viceroy 093
  Room rates:
  double, from AED430
  Yas Marina
  Abu Dhabi
  T 2656 0000
  www.viceroyhotelsandresorts.com

WALLPAPER* CITY GUIDES

Executive Editor
Rachael Moloney

Author
Warren Singh-Bartlett

Art Editor
Eriko Shimazaki
Designer
Mayumi Hashimoto
Map Illustrator
Russell Bell

Photography Editor
Elisa Merlo
Assistant Photography Editor
Nabil Butt

Chief Sub-Editor
Nick Mee
Sub-Editor
Farah Shafiq

Editorial Assistant
Emilee Jane Tombs

Interns
Harriet Ball
Enrica Casentini

Wallpaper* Group Editor-in-Chief
Tony Chambers
Publishing Director
Gord Ray
Managing Editor
Oliver Adamson

Original Design
Loran Stosskopf

Wallpaper* ® is a
registered trademark
of IPC Media Limited

First published 2007
Revised and updated
2011 and 2014

All prices are correct at
the time of going to press,
but are subject to change.

Printed in China

PHAIDON

Phaidon Press Limited
Regent's Wharf
All Saints Street
London N1 9PA

Phaidon Press Inc
65 Bleecker Street
New York, NY 10012

Phaidon® is a registered
trademark of Phaidon
Press Limited

www.phaidon.com

A CIP Catalogue record for
this book is available from
the British Library.

© 2007, 2011 and 2014
IPC Media Limited

ISBN 978 0 7148 6825 7

PHOTOGRAPHERS

Nagib Khazaka
Dubai Marina, pp010-011
Jumeirah Emirates
Towers, p012
InterContinental Festival
City, p026, p027
Al Ahmadiya, p036, p037
Pierchic, p044, p045
Okku, pp048-049
Reflets par Pierre
Gagnaire, p057
The Roof Top, pp058-059
Zuma, pp60-061
Burj Khalifa, p065
The Gate, pp066-067
O' de Rose, p073
Meydan Racecourse,
pp084-085

Raymond Meier
Imam Mosque, p096
Friday Mosque, p097

**Courtesy of Museum of
Islamic Art**
Museum of Islamic Art,
p089, pp090-091

Mai Nordahn
Clock Tower
Roundabout, pp014-015
XVA Art Hotel, p017
Indego, p051
Dubai Creek Golf & Yacht
Club, pp070-071
Amara, p081
Ski Dubai, pp086-087

Walter Shintani
Dubai city view,
inside front cover
Park Hyatt, p022
The Archive, p033
Ayyam, pp034-035
Comptoir 102, p041,
pp042-043
MAKE Business Hub, p046
THE One, p047
The Farm, p050
MusicHall, p052, p053
The Pantry, pp054-055
La Serre, p056
Tima Ouzden, p063
Cayan Tower, p068
The Index, p069
Kasa, p074
Boutique 1, pp076-077
SPM, pp078-079

Jonathan de Villiers
Burj Al Arab, p013

DUBAI
A COLOUR-CODED GUIDE TO THE HOT 'HOODS

MARINA
This high-rise neighbourhood is the cultural and leisure counterweight to Sheikh Zayed

SHEIKH ZAYED
Dubai's glittering-glass business district also boasts many fine-dining and nightlife venues

DOWNTOWN
Home to the tallest building in the world, Downtown is fast becoming the city's nucleus

DEIRA
The tumbledown chaos of the real old town is a bustling reminder of Dubai's first boom

AL QUOZ
Art galleries and ateliers have added a more creative edge to this gritty industrial zone

BUR DUBAI
There's a hotchpotch of heritage architecture and Indian restaurants in this 1960s 'burb

JUMEIRAH
Explore the boutiques, cafés and spas set back from this stretch of beachside playground

CREEK
An expanse of freshwater that's home to a wildlife sanctuary, two golf clubs and a park

For a full description of each neighbourhood, see the Introduction.
Featured venues are colour-coded, according to the district in which they are located.